TOP HITS OF 2013

WITHDRAWN

ISBN 978-1-4803-5487-6

HAL•LEONARD®
CORPORATION
7777 W. BLUEMOUND RD. P.O. BOX 13819 MILWAUKEE, WI 53213

Visit Hal Leonard Online at
www.halleonard.com

BLURRED LINES

Words and Music by PHARRELL WILLIAMS
and ROBIN THICKE

Moderate groove

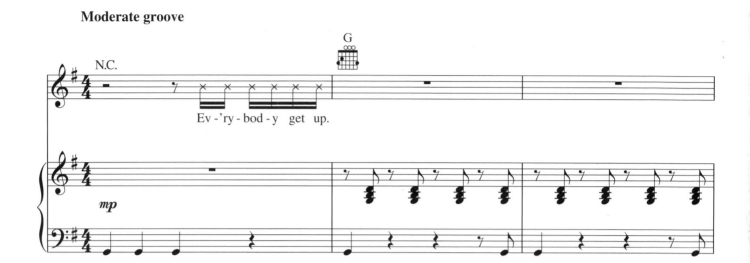

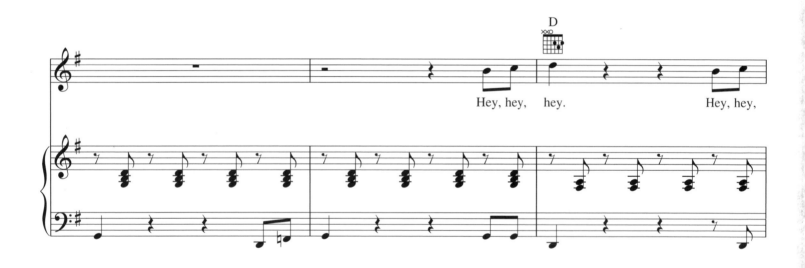

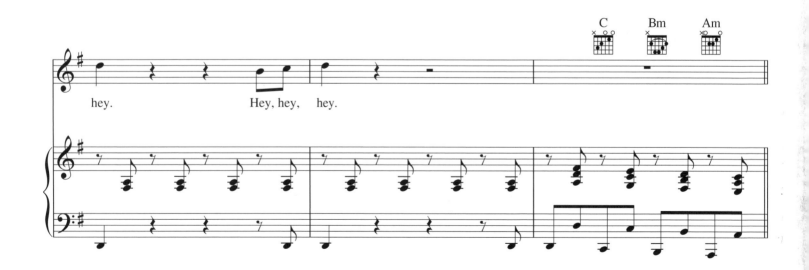

Additional Lyrics

Rap: One thing I ask of you, let me be the one you back that ass to.
Yo, from Malibu to Paribu, yeah, had a bitch, but she ain't bad as you.
So, hit me up when you pass through, I give you something big enough to tear your ass in two.
Swag on 'em even when you dress casual. I mean, it's almost unbearable.
In a hundred year, not dare would I pull a Pharcide bitch, you pass me by.
I'm nothing like your last guy, he too square for you. He don't smack that ass and pull your hair for you.
So I'm just watchin' and waitin' for you to salute the truly pimpin'.
Not many women can refuse this pimpin'. I'm a nice guy, but don't get it confused, you gettin' it.

CRUISE

Words and Music by CHASE RICE,
TYLER HUBBARD, BRIAN KELLEY,
JOEY MOI and JESSE RICE

Moderately fast

Ba - by, you a song. You make me wan - na roll __ my win - dows down and

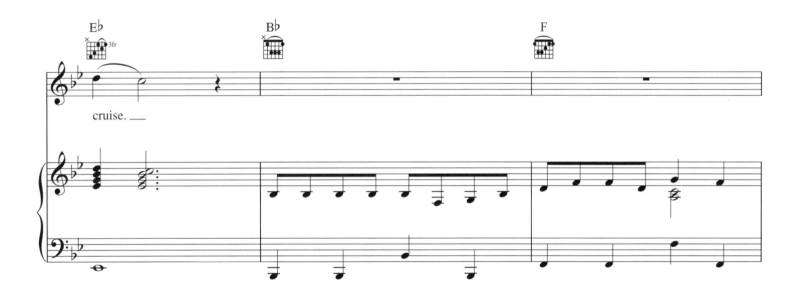

cruise. __

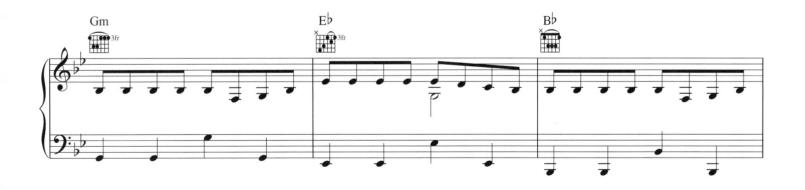

CALL ME MAYBE

Words and Music by CARLY RAE JEPSEN,
JOSHUA RAMSAY and TAVISH CROWE

Moderate Pop

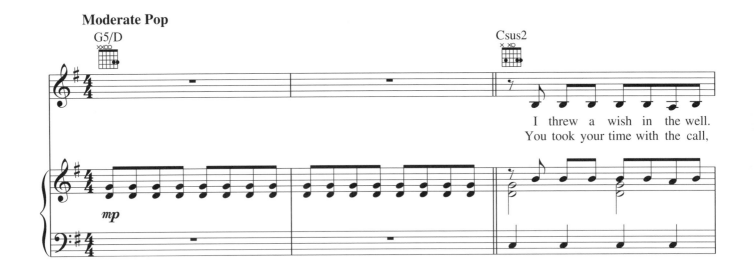

I threw a wish in the well.
You took your time with the call,

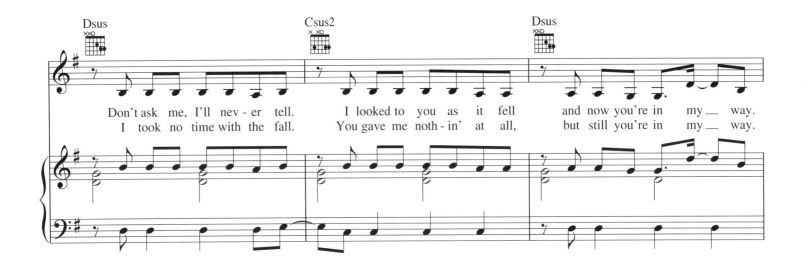

Don't ask me, I'll nev-er tell.   I looked to you as it fell   and now you're in   my __ way.
I took no time with the fall.   You gave me noth-in' at all,   but still you're in   my __ way.

I trade my soul for a wish,   pen-nies and dimes for a kiss.   I was-n't look-in' for this,
I beg and bor-row and steal,   at first sight and it's real.   I did-n't know I would feel

CATCH MY BREATH

Words and Music by KELLY CLARKSON,
JASON HALBERT and ERIC OLSON

* *Sung as written both times.*

DAYLIGHT

Words and Music by ADAM LEVINE,
MAX MARTIN, SAM MARTIN
and MASON LEVY

Here I am, wait-ing, __ I'll have to leave soon. __ Why am I

hold-ing on? We knew this day would come, __ we knew it all a-long. __

How did it come so fast? __ This is our __ last night, __

I WILL WAIT

Words and Music by
MUMFORD & SONS

GET LUCKY

Words and Music by THOMAS BANGALTER,
GUY MANUEL HOMEM CHRISTO, PHARRELL WILLIAMS
and NILE RODGERS

GONE, GONE, GONE

Words and Music by GREGG WATTENBERG,
DEREK FUHRMANN and TODD CLARK

Moderately fast

When

life leaves __ you high and dry, I'll be at ___ your door to-night if

you need __ help, ___ if you need __ help. ___ I'll

Recorded a half step higher.

don't stop beat - in'.   Like a drum, ba - by, don't stop beat - in'.

Like a drum, ba - by, don't stop beat - in'.   Like a drum, my heart

nev - er stops beat- in' for you.   And long af - ter you're gone,   gone,

F5   F/A   G7sus

F5   F5   F/A   G7sus   F5

gone,   I'll love you long af - ter you're gone,   gone,   gone.

rit.

HEART ATTACK

Words and Music by JASON EVIGAN, MITCH ALLAN,
SEAN DOUGLAS, NIKKI WILLIAMS, AARON PHILLIPS
and DEMI LOVATO

Put-tin' my de-fens-es up 'cause I don't wan-na fall in love. If I

ev-er did that, I think I'd have a heart at - tack. _____

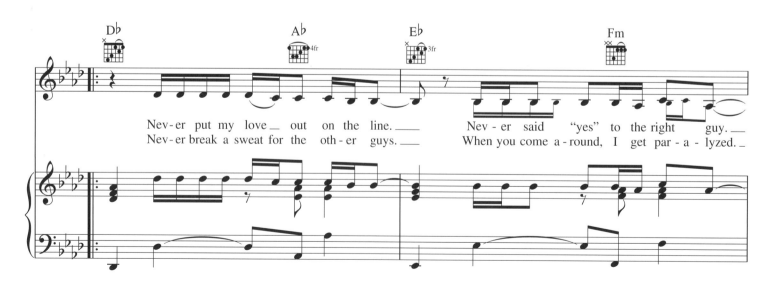

Nev-er put my love _ out on the line. _____ Nev-er said "yes" to the right guy. _____
Nev-er break a sweat for the oth-er guys. _____ When you come a-round, I get par-a-lyzed. _

IT'S A BEAUTIFUL DAY

Words and Music by MICHAEL BUBLÉ,
ALAN CHANG and AMY FOSTER

JUST GIVE ME A REASON

Words and Music by ALECIA MOORE,
JEFF BHASKER and NATE RUESS

78

MIRRORS

Words and Music by JUSTIN TIMBERLAKE,
JAMES FAUNTLEROY, JEROME HARMON,
TIM MOSLEY, CHRIS GODBEY and GARLAND MOSLEY

Aren't you some-

NEXT TO ME

Words and Music by EMELI SANDÉ,
HARRY CRAZE, HUGO CHEGWIN
and ANUP PAUL

You won't find __ him drink-ing un-der ta - bles,

mon-ey's spent __ and all my friends have van - ished,

and I can't

roll - ing dice and stay - ing out till three.

seem to find no help or love till for free,

You won't ev - er find __ him be-ing un-faith - ful. You will find __

I know there's no need __ for me to pan - ic. 'Cause I'll find __

RADIOACTIVE

Words and Music by DANIEL REYNOLDS,
BENJAMIN McKEE, DANIEL SERMON,
ALEXANDER GRANT and JOSH MOSSER

WE CAN'T STOP

Words and Music by MILEY CYRUS,
MICHAEL WILLIAMS, PIERRE SLAUGHTER,
TIMOTHY THOMAS, THERON THOMAS,
DOUGLAS DAVIS and RICKY WALTERS

Moderately slow groove

It's our par-ty, we can do what we want. It's our par-ty, we can say what we want.

It's our par-ty, we can love who we want. We can kiss who we want. We can screw who we want.

Red cups and sweat-y bod-ies ev-'ry-where, _____ hands in the air like we don't_ care,_____

C#5   A5

things, they don't run we. Don't take noth-in' from no-bod-y, yeah, __ yeah. __

E   G#m7

It's our par-ty, we can do what we want. It's our par-ty, we can say what we want.

C#m7   Asus2   **To Coda** ⊕

It's our par-ty, we can love who we want. We can kiss who we want. We can screw who we want.

E   G#m

To my home girls here with the big __ butt, ___ shak-in' it like we at a strip __ club, ___

STAY

Words and Music by MIKKY EKKO
and JUSTIN PARKER

Moderate Ballad

TRY

Words and Music by busbee
and BEN WEST

WHEN I WAS YOUR MAN

Words and Music by BRUNO MARS,
ARI LEVINE, PHILIP LAWRENCE
and ANDREW WYATT